Series Science and Technologies

To all my teachers who put up with me
and to all my students whom I have supported.

Giorgio Patuelli Tomba

The Dawn of Artificial Intelligence
Understanding and Navigating the Digital Future

Ark59 Media

Those who wish to stay updated on the author's books and activities can visit the website: www.giorgiopatuelli.it

ISBN 979-83-10-67923-8

Self-produced in February 2025 at the Atelier Ark59-Design by Giorgio Patuelli in Imola, Bologna, Italy

Indice

	Prologue	4
0	"Human" Intelligence?	5
1	What is Artificial Intelligence?	9
2	How Artificial Intelligence Works	13
3	Applications of Artificial Intelligence Today	21
4	AI and Art: Digital Creativity	24
5	The Ethics of Artificial Intelligence	33
6	The Possible Futures of Artificial Intelligence	39
7	AI in Italy: State and Perspectives	49
8	Creating with AI: Opportunities for Innovators and Artists	57
9	Philosophical Implications of Artificial Intelligence	65
10	Practical Guide for Those Who Want to Approach AI	73
11	Leonardo Visual Innovator	83
12	Final Reflections on the Impact of Artificial Intelligence	89
	Appendix	
	Glossary of Key Terms	95
	List of Recommended Resources	97
	Final Thoughts	100

Prologue

Artificial intelligence is one of the most revolutionary innovations of our time, destined to profoundly transform every aspect of our lives. As an architect, sculptor, and artist, I have always sought to explore the intersection between "human creativity" and technology.

Isn't it true, after all, that the Latin word ars, from which "art" derives, has, albeit indirectly, its roots in the Greek word τέχνη (téchnē)?

My training has taught me how abstract ideas, through design, can take concrete form, and now, with the advent of artificial intelligence, I see the possibility of a new dimension of expression and innovation.

This book arises from the desire to explore and share the extraordinary potential of artificial intelligence.
It is not just a technology but a true paradigm shift that will influence how we think, create, and live.

Through these chapters, I aim to guide the reader on a journey that begins with the fundamentals of AI and ventures into its most creative and innovative applications.

My motivation is twofold: on the one hand, I want to provide those who are interested with a simple and clear explanation of its fundamental concepts and practical applications.
On the other, I wish to inspire artists, creatives, and innovators to view AI not as a threat but as an opportunity to expand their horizons and create new forms of expression.

We live in an era where machines are no longer merely tools but creative partners capable of expanding our abilities and offering us new perspectives, freeing us from a host of tedious tasks.

This book is an invitation to explore this new frontier together—with curiosity and an open mind—to understand how artificial intelligence can enrich our lives and work.

Chapter 0

"Human" Intelligence?

Human, or natural, intelligence is one of the most fascinating and complex qualities that defines the human being.

It has been the subject of study and debate by philosophers and scientists for centuries, as they have sought to understand its dynamics and implications. Historically, intelligence has been considered the ability to learn, comprehend, adapt, and solve problems.
Thinkers in ancient Greece, such as Plato and Aristotle, viewed intelligence as a fundamental part of the rational soul—an element that elevated humans above the animal kingdom, enabling them to contemplate abstract concepts and seek truth.

In more modern times, the French philosopher René Descartes, perhaps better known by his Latinized name, Cartesius, contributed to the definition of human intelligence as the ability to think. His famous statement, "Ego cogito, ergo sum, sive existo"—"I think, therefore I am, or rather I exist"—underscored that the capacity for reflection and self-awareness defines the essence of humanity.

Immanuel Kant also shaped the modern understanding of intelligence, arguing that humans possess an intelligence capable not only of understanding the world through the senses but also of engaging in moral reasoning and critical judgment.

From a scientific perspective, neuroscience has made strides in unraveling the cognitive processes of the human brain.
Researchers like Howard Gardner, with his theory of "multiple intelligences," have proposed that human intelligence is not monolithic but consists of diverse forms, including logical-mathematical, linguistic, musical, spatial, and interpersonal intelligence, among others.

This pluralistic approach has transformed how we view intelligence, broadening our perspective beyond traditional measures like IQ (intelligence quotient).

Human intelligence, unlike artificial intelligence, is not solely based on the processing of information and algorithms.
It is deeply influenced by emotions, empathy, and interaction with social and cultural contexts. These dimensions of our "natural" or perhaps better, "human" intelligence raise philosophical questions about whether it can ever be fully replicated by artificial intelligence. Such questions touch on the very essence of what it means to be "intelligent" in the human sense of the term.

Thus, a more fitting name for artificial intelligence might be "computational intelligence." This term highlights the fact that AI operates through computational processes—complex algorithms and calculations—rather than the creativity or self-awareness characteristic of human intelligence.

The phrase "computational intelligence" emphasizes its ability to process and analyze data, make predictions, and solve problems, avoiding confusion with human or natural intelligence, which is intertwined with emotions, self-awareness, and a profound understanding of the world..

www.giorgiopatuelli.it

"The measure of intelligence is the ability to change."

Albert Einstein

"The measure of intelligence is the ability to safeguard

the environment we live in."

Porifera

Chapter 1

What is Artificial Intelligence?

Definition and Key Concepts

Artificial Intelligence (AI) is a branch of computer science focused on creating machines and software capable of performing tasks that would typically require human intelligence.

These tasks include, but are not limited to, speech recognition, natural language understanding, computer vision, and decision-making.

The primary goal of AI is to develop systems that can perform these functions autonomously, adapt to new information, and improve their performance over time.

Artificial intelligence can be divided into various subcategories, including machine learning, deep learning, and computer vision. Machine learning, in particular, is a technique that allows computers to "learn" from examples without being explicitly programmed to perform a specific task. This is achieved through analyzing large amounts of data, from which AI systems can extract patterns and make predictions.

History and Development of AI: From Its Origins to Recent Advances

The history of artificial intelligence dates back several decades, with roots in early philosophical and mathematical ideas about intelligence and computation. However, modern AI took shape only in the mid-20th century.
One of the first major contributions to the field of AI came from the British mathematician Alan Turing. In the 1950s, Turing proposed the

idea of a "universal machine," now known as the Turing machine, capable of performing any computation if correctly programmed. Turing is also known for formulating the famous "Turing Test," a thought experiment to determine whether a machine can exhibit intelligent behavior indistinguishable from that of a human. Notably, Turing also played a key role in decrypting the Nazi Enigma machine during World War II, which had previously been used to send undecipherable messages.

The term "artificial intelligence" was coined in 1956 by John McCarthy during the famous Dartmouth conference. This event is considered the formal birth of AI as an academic field of study. In the decades that followed, AI experienced periods of great enthusiasm as well as phases of disappointment, known as "AI winters," when progress failed to meet expectations.

In the 1980s and 1990s, AI gained new momentum with the development of artificial neural networks, which mimic the functioning of the human brain to solve complex problems. However, it wasn't until the 21st century, with the increase in computer processing power and the availability of large amounts of data, that AI reached extraordinary levels of performance, marking an era of rapid advances in fields like deep learning and computer vision.

Differences Between Narrow AI, General AI, and Superintelligence

In the field of artificial intelligence, it is important to distinguish between different levels of capability and application. Currently, most AI applications fall into the category of narrow AI, but there are concepts and theories regarding more advanced forms of AI.

Narrow (Weak) AI

Narrow AI is designed to perform a single task or a limited set of very specific tasks. A classic example is an AI system that plays chess. This type of AI can outperform human capabilities in well-defined tasks, but it has no understanding or capability beyond the functions it was programmed for. Voice assistants like Siri or Alexa, which can answer questions or execute simple commands, are examples of narrow AI.

General (Strong) AI

General AI is a form of artificial intelligence that would be capable of understanding, learning, and applying knowledge to a wide range of tasks, much like a human being. This form of AI does not yet exist, but it is a long-term goal for many researchers in the field. General AI would be able to transfer skills learned in one area to another and tackle new, unfamiliar problems without needing to be reprogrammed.

Superintelligence

Superintelligence is a theoretical concept referring to an artificial intelligence that far surpasses human intelligence in nearly every field, including creativity, problem-solving, and social skills. This concept is often discussed in philosophical and futuristic contexts, as superintelligence could represent one of humanity's greatest challenges and opportunities. While general AI would operate at a human level of intelligence, superintelligence would go beyond, with capabilities difficult to predict.

In summary, artificial intelligence exists in various forms and levels of complexity. From narrow AI, which is already widely used today, to general AI, which represents an as-yet-unreached frontier, to superintelligence, which remains within the realm of theory, AI continues to be a dynamic and evolving field with an increasing impact on our society.

Alan Turing   *Test di Turing*   *John McCarthy*

Neural algorithms

Chapter 2

How Artificial Intelligence Works

Machine Learning Algorithms

Machine learning is one of the fundamental pillars of modern artificial intelligence. It is a methodology that allows computers to learn and improve their performance through experience, without being explicitly programmed to perform a specific task. In other words, machine learning systems analyze large amounts of data to identify patterns and make predictions or decisions based on those patterns.

How Do Machine Learning Algorithms Work?
Machine learning algorithms operate through an iterative process that can be summarized in three main phases:

Phase 1: Data CollectionThe first step is to gather a large dataset relevant to the problem at hand. This data can take various forms, such as numbers, text, images, or
sounds. It's essential to remember that, fundamentally, this data consists of simple binary signals—essentially, ones and zeros (on/off).

Phase 2: Training the Model
The algorithms use this data to "train" themselves by identifying patterns and relationships within the data. During this phase, the model is exposed to input data and learns to produce the desired output.

Phase 3: Testing and Improvement
Once trained, the model is tested on new data to evaluate its performance. Based on the results, the model is iteratively refined and improved in successive stages to increase its accuracy and effectiveness.
Types of Machine Learning
There are several types of machine learning, each suited to specific types of problems.

Supervised Learning

In this approach, the model is trained using a dataset that includes both inputs and the desired outputs. The goal is for the model to learn how to predict the correct output given a new input. Common examples include classifying emails as "spam" or "not spam," or predicting real estate prices.

Unsupervised Learning

Here, the model works with unlabeled data and tries to identify hidden patterns or structures within the data. This type of learning is often used for clustering, where the model groups similar data points together. An example would be segmenting markets based on consumer behavior.

Reinforcement Learning

In this case, the model learns through a system of rewards and penalties. The model takes actions in an environment and receives positive or negative feedback based on the outcomes of its actions. It adjusts its behavior to maximize total rewards. This approach is used in fields such as robotics and video games.

Practical Applications of Machine Learning Algorithms

Machine learning algorithms have a wide range of applications in everyday life:

Speech and Natural Language Recognition

Virtual assistants like Siri and Alexa use machine learning to understand and respond to user requests.

Recommendation Systems

Platforms like Netflix and Amazon use these algorithms to suggest movies, TV shows, or products based on user preferences and past behavior.

Fraud Detection

Banks and credit card companies use machine learning to identify suspicious transactions by analyzing patterns in transaction data.

Medical Diagnosis

Algorithms can help identify diseases by analyzing medical images or patient data, assisting doctors in making clinical decisions.

QNeural Networks and Deep Learning

Neural networks are computational models inspired by the structure and functioning of the human brain—at least to the extent of current knowledge. They form the foundation of deep learning, a subcategory of machine learning that has driven significant advancements in artificial intelligence in recent years.

What Are Neural Networks?

A neural network consists of layers of interconnected units called artificial neurons, which process information through weighted connections. Each neuron receives input, processes it by applying a mathematical function, and transmits the output to subsequent neurons. This process allows the network to learn complex data representations and perform sophisticated tasks, such as image recognition or machine translation.

Deep Learning

Deep learning refers to neural networks with multiple hidden layers, enabling the model to learn data representations at different levels of abstraction. These deep networks are particularly effective in processing seemingly unstructured data, such as images, audio, and text.

Types of Neural Networks in Deep Learning

There are various types of neural networks used in deep learning, each suited to specific applications.

Convolutional Neural Networks (CNNs)

Primarily used for image and video recognition, CNNs are designed to identify spatial patterns and local features in visual data. Common applications include facial recognition, medical diagnosis through imaging, and autonomous driving.

Recurrent Neural Networks (RNNs)

These networks are ideal for processing sequential data like text and audio, as they maintain a memory of previous inputs through internal loops. RNNs are used in applications such as machine translation, speech recognition, and text generation.

Generative Adversarial Networks (GANs)

GANs consist of two networks that compete with each other: one generates new data similar to the training data, while the other attempts to distinguish between real and generated data. This approach is used to create highly realistic synthetic images, videos, and audio.

Neural Network Training Process

Training a neural network involves optimizing the weights of the connections between the "neurons" so the network can produce accurate outputs. This process consists of the following steps:

Forward Pass

The input data is processed through the network layer by layer until it produces an output.

Neural Network Training Process

Training a neural network involves optimizing the weights of the connections between the "neurons" so the network can produce accurate outputs. This process includes the following steps:

Forward Pass
The input data is processed through the network layer by layer until an output is produced.

Backward Pass: Backpropagation
The error is propagated backward through the network, and the weights are updated using optimization algorithms such as gradient descent to minimize the error.

Iteration
This process is repeated across many data samples until the network achieves a satisfactory level of accuracy.

Challenges and Considerations in Deep Learning
Despite the success of deep learning, there are several challenges associated with this approach:

High Data Requirements
Deep neural networks require vast amounts of data to be effectively trained, which can be a limitation in some domains.

High Computational Cost
Training deep networks demands significant computational resources and time.
Interpretability: The decisions made by neural networks are often difficult to interpret, which can pose challenges in critical applications such as healthcare or finance.

Data Is the Fuel of AI
Data is essential for the effective functioning of artificial intelligence. Without high-quality data, machine learning algorithms and neural networks cannot learn accurately or effectively.

The Importance of Data in AI
Data provides the necessary information for AI models to recognize patterns, make predictions, and make informed decisions. The quantity, quality, and diversity of data directly affect the performance and reliability of AI systems.

Types of Data Used in AI
Structured Data: Information organized into predefined formats, such as database tables, which are easily interpretable by algorithms.

Unstructured Data
Unstructured data refers to information not organized according to a predefined schema, such as text, images, audio, and video. These types of data often require preprocessing and advanced techniques to be used effectively.

Data Collection and Preparation
The process of collecting and preparing data involves several stages:

Data Acquisition:
Collecting data from various sources, such as databases, sensors, the web, and human interactions.

Data Annotation:
Labeling the data, particularly in supervised learning, to provide models with the necessary information for learning.

Data Splitting:
Dividing the data into training, validation, and test sets to train and properly evaluate the models.
Challenges Related to Data in AI

Data Quality
Working with accurate, high-quality data is essential. If the data used is imprecise or low-quality, the AI models created may become ineffective or even misleading, leading to incorrect conclusions.

Bias in Data
Bias, or prejudice present in the initial dataset, is a critical concern. If the data used to train the models contain biases or distorted representations, the models may perpetuate or amplify these biases in their decisions. This is particularly concerning in sensitive social and cultural contexts.

Privacy and Security
When collecting and using data, it is crucial to comply with privacy regulations and ensure sensitive information is protected. Data security is a priority to avoid risks related to exposure or misuse of data.

Managing Large Data Volumes
Handling vast amounts of data requires appropriate infrastructures and technologies. Ensuring that these are efficient and fast is critical to processing large datasets without compromising quality or accuracy.

Strategies for Effective Data Management
Data Governance: Implementing policies and procedures that ensure data quality, security, and ethical usage. This includes clear rules on how data should be managed and utilized.

Big Data Technologies
Using tools and platforms that enable the efficient management and

processing of large amounts of data is crucial for obtaining reliable and timely results.

Data Augmentation
This technique increases the quantity and variety of available data, for example, by creating new data instances from existing ones. This enhances the models' ability to learn and generalize effectively.

Collaboration and Data Sharing
Collaborations between different organizations to share data and resources can lead to the development of more robust and comprehensive models capable of addressing complex challenges.

Conclusion
Data is the heart of artificial intelligence. Knowing how to collect, manage, and effectively utilize large volumes of data is essential for developing powerful and reliable AI systems. Understanding the importance of data and tackling the challenges related to its management are fundamental to fully leveraging AI's potential to solve complex problems and improve society.

Algorithms

It takes something more than
intelligence to act intelligently.

Fëdor Dostoevskij

Chapter 3

Applications of Artificial Intelligence Today

Artificial intelligence is no longer just a theoretical concept or experimental technology; it has become an integral part of numerous industries, revolutionizing the way we work, live, and interact with the world. In this chapter, we will explore the main applications of AI in the fields of healthcare, finance, manufacturing, and services, as well as in our daily lives. Additionally, we will examine some success stories that demonstrate the tangible impact of AI.

Healthcare, Finance, Manufacturing, and Services Sectors

Healthcare
In the healthcare sector, AI is making significant improvements in diagnosis, treatment, and patient management. AI algorithms can analyze vast amounts of medical data, including images, lab tests, and medical records, to assist doctors in diagnosing diseases more accurately and prompt

Key Examples

Image Diagnosis
Deep learning algorithms are used to analyze medical images such as X-rays, MRIs, and CT scans. These systems can detect abnormalities that might go unnoticed by the human eye, enabling earlier diagnosis of conditions like cancer.

Virtual Assistance
AI-based healthcare assistants, such as chatbots and mobile apps, provide support to patients by answering questions, monitoring symptoms, and sending medication reminders.

Finance
The financial sector was among the first to adopt AI, leveraging its ability to analyze large volumes of data in real-time and make quick, informed decisions.

Common Applications

Algorithmic Trading
AI is used to analyze financial markets and execute automatic trading operations. These algorithms can monitor markets 24/7, identify investment opportunities, and respond faster than any human trader.

Risk Management
Banks and insurance companies use AI to evaluate the risk associated with loans, investments, and insurance policies. This enables better decision-making and more personalized offers for customers.

Fraud Detection
AI algorithms analyze financial transactions in real-time to detect suspicious activities. When anomalies, such as unexpected transactions, are identified, the system can block the operation or alert the customer.

Manufacturing
In manufacturing, AI is improving efficiency, quality, and operational safety. Smart factories leverage AI to optimize production and minimize downtime.

Key Innovations

Predictive Maintenance
AI algorithms monitor machinery in real-time and predict when maintenance is needed. This reduces unplanned downtime and extends the life of equipment.

Automation in Production
AI automates complex and repetitive processes, boosting productivity and reducing human error. Advanced robots equipped with AI can perform tasks such as assembly, quality control, and packaging.

Supply Chain Optimization
AI helps companies manage supply chains more efficiently by predicting demand, optimizing inventories, and planning shipments to cut costs and improve customer service.

Services
AI is also transforming the service sector, enhancing customer experiences and optimizing business operations.

Popular Use Cases:
Customer Service
AI-powered chatbots and virtual assistants are increasingly used to answer customer queries, resolve issues, and handle requests. These systems operate 24/7, offering instant assistance and reducing wait times.

Marketing Personalization
Companies use AI to analyze customer data and tailor marketing campaigns. Algorithms identify products and services customers are most likely to purchase and send targeted offers, improving campaign effectiveness.

Logistics and Resource Management
Logistics companies use AI to optimize delivery routes, manage inventories, and improve resource planning. This reduces operational costs and increases efficiency.

AI in Daily Life: Virtual Assistants, Smart Homes, and More

AI is not confined to the corporate or scientific world; it is increasingly present in our daily lives, enhancing the comfort and efficiency of our routines.

Virtual Assistants
Virtual assistants like Siri, Alexa, and Google Assistant have become integral to our daily lives. These AI-powered systems can perform a wide variety of tasks, such as answering questions, managing calendars, sending messages, controlling smart home devices, and more. With their ability to understand natural language and learn from user interactions, these assistants are becoming increasingly personalized and proactive.

Smart Home
Smart homes are revolutionizing the way we live and manage our households. Intelligent home devices, such as thermostats, lights, locks, and security systems, can be controlled and automated using AI.

Smart Thermostats
These devices can learn a family's habits and automatically adjust the temperature to optimize comfort and energy efficiency.

Security Systems
Smart cameras use AI to recognize faces, identify suspicious movements, and send real-time alerts to homeowners.

Home Assistance
Robotic vacuum cleaners and other cleaning devices use artificial intelligence to navigate homes and clean autonomously, adapting to different surfaces and obstacles.

Entertainment and Media
AI has significantly influenced the way we consume media and entertainment. Streaming platforms like Netflix, Spotify, and YouTube use artificial intelligence algorithms to suggest content based on user preferences, making the experience more personalized and engaging.

Navigation and Transportation
Navigation applications such as Google Maps and Waze use AI to analyze real-time traffic data and provide optimized routes. Furthermore, artificial intelligence is driving the development of autonomous vehicles, which have the potential to revolutionize transportation by reducing accidents and improving mobility.

Success Case Studies
To better understand the impact of artificial intelligence, let's explore some success stories that demonstrate how AI is already making a difference across various industries.

Google DeepMind and AlphaGo
One of the most renowned cases is the success of AlphaGo, a program developed by Google DeepMind that defeated the world's best human players in Go, an ancient strategy game considered far more complex than chess. AlphaGo used deep neural networks and reinforcement learning techniques to learn to play at a superhuman level, marking a historic milestone in AI. This achievement demonstrated the potential of

AI to solve complex problems and paved the way for new applications in various fields.

IBM Watson in Medicine

IBM Watson is another notable example of artificial intelligence applied to medicine. Watson has been used to analyze vast amounts of clinical data and provide personalized treatment recommendations for cancer patients. In some cases, Watson identified treatment options that human doctors had not considered, improving patient outcomes and showcasing AI's potential to support critical medical decision-making.

Tesla and Autonomous Driving

Tesla is a pioneer in developing autonomous vehicles. The company leverages AI to power its self-driving system, enabling Tesla cars to navigate public roads autonomously. While fully autonomous driving is not yet commonplace, Tesla's advancements highlight how AI is transforming the automotive industry, bringing us closer to a future where driverless vehicles could become the norm.

Amazon and Logistics

Amazon has integrated artificial intelligence into numerous aspects of its supply chain and logistics operations. Amazon warehouses use intelligent robots to move products, optimizing inventory management and improving operational efficiency. Furthermore, AI powers Amazon's recommendation system, which suggests personalized products to customers, increasing sales and enhancing the shopping experience.

Netflix and Personalized Recommendations

Netflix is well-known for its AI-powered recommendation system, which suggests movies and TV shows based on user preferences. This system is critical to the platform's success, as it helps keep users engaged and satisfied with the content offered. The AI analyzes users' viewing behaviors and uses this data to predict what they might enjoy watching in the future.

Conclusion

Artificial intelligence has become an essential component of many key sectors, with applications that improve our health, optimize business operations, personalize our daily experiences, and even revolutionize transportation. Success stories such as AlphaGo, IBM Watson, Tesla, Amazon, and Netflix not only highlight AI's potential but also demonstrate its tangible impact on our daily lives and the future of society.

As AI continues to evolve, we can expect to witness even more innovations that will shape our world in ways we cannot yet imagine. However, with these powerful capabilities also come new challenges that we must approach with care and responsibility.

Healthcare

Bias

Chapter 4

AI and Art: Digital Creativity

AI in Artistic Creation: Painting, Music, Writing, and Design
Artificial intelligence is rapidly transforming the artistic landscape,
opening up new possibilities for creation and creative expression. AI is
no longer just a tool for automating repetitive tasks; it has become a
partner in the creation of art, music, and literary works. This technologi-
cal revolution challenges our traditional ideas about what it means to be
an artist and where creativity resides, sparking significant discussions
about copyright and intellectual property.

AI-Generated Painting
In the field of painting, AI has demonstrated its ability to create visual
works that rival those of human artists. Using neural networks and
machine learning algorithms, AI can analyze and replicate existing
artistic styles or even generate entirely new ones.

One famous example is The Next Rembrandt, a project that used AI to
create a painting in the style of the renowned Dutch artist Rembrandt. By
analyzing hundreds of Rembrandt's works, the AI synthesized a new
portrait that looked as if it had come straight from the master's own
hands.

Generative Adversarial Networks (GANs) are particularly powerful in
creating artistic images. These networks operate in pairs: one network,
the "generator," creates new images, while the other, the "discriminator,"
evaluates their quality. Through this iterative process, the AI becomes
increasingly adept at producing realistic or stylistically coherent images.
Contemporary artists are beginning to collaborate with these technologies, producing hybrid works that combine human vision with the computational power of AI.

AI-Generated Music
Artificial intelligence is also revolutionizing music creation. Deep learning algorithms can analyze thousands of musical compositions, learning the harmonic, melodic, and rhythmic structures that define a particular style or genre. With this knowledge, AI can compose new pieces of music that adhere to genre conventions or, in some cases, explore novel sonic combinations.

One notable example is AIVA (Artificial Intelligence Virtual Artist), an AI designed to compose classical music. AIVA has been trained on an extensive repertoire of classical works and is now capable of producing original compositions that have been used in films, video games, and advertisements. In the realm of pop and electronic music, AI is increasingly becoming a creative collaborator, assisting producers in generating beats, melodies, and arrangements that enhance the human creative process.

AI in Writing and Literature
Writing is another area where AI is making a significant impact. Advanced natural language processing (NLP) algorithms can generate texts ranging from news articles to short stories and even poetry. These systems analyze vast amounts of text, understanding context, syntax, and tone, and then use this knowledge to produce new content.

One example is GPT-4, a language model developed by OpenAI, capable of writing articles, stories, and even screenplays. GPT-4 can mimic the writing style of various authors and produce texts that, in many cases, are indistinguishable from those written by humans. However, the use of AI in writing raises important questions about originality and intellectual property, as AI-generated texts are based on preexisting data and not on personal experience or human emotion.

Conclusion
AI in artistic creation represents a fascinating intersection of technology and creativity. While artificial intelligence lacks consciousness or emotion to guide its artistic output, it can still generate works that surprise, inspire, and provoke thought. As these technologies continue to advance, we are likely to see an increasing number of collaborations between human artists and machines, leading to new forms of expression and a continual redefinition of what we consider art.

Doubt is one of the names of intelligence.

Jorge Luis Borges

The problem with humanity is that stupid people are always very sure, while intelligent people are full of doubts.

Bertrand Russell

Chapter 5

The Ethics of Artificial Intelligence

Artificial intelligence is profoundly transforming our society, offering extraordinary opportunities but also raising significant ethical dilemmas. As AI becomes more powerful and pervasive, crucial questions emerge about how this technology should be used, who benefits from it, and what risks it poses. In this chapter, we will explore the main ethical challenges related to AI, focusing on issues such as bias and discrimination, privacy and security, and the impact of AI on the workforce.

Ethical Dilemmas Related to AI
Bias, Discrimination, and Automated Decisions
One of the primary ethical dilemmas in artificial intelligence revolves around bias and discrimination in automated systems. Bias, in this context, refers to the tendency to produce distorted outcomes due to unrepresentative training data or human prejudices. Although AI systems are designed to be objective, they often mirror the biases present in the data they are trained on. This can result in unfair or discriminatory decisions, particularly in sensitive areas such as employment, criminal justice, and access to financial services.

Bias in Training Data

Bias can manifest in various ways. For instance, if an AI system is trained on historical data reflecting racial or gender biases, it is likely to perpetuate those biases in its decisions. A notable example is AI algorithms used in hiring processes, which may unintentionally penalize candidates from minority groups if the historical data includes prejudiced trends.

Additionally, bias can arise from a lack of representativeness in training data. If an algorithm is trained on datasets that fail to adequately represent all demographics or contexts in which it will be applied, it may make inaccurate or unfair predictions for certain populations. For example, facial recognition systems have been shown to be less accurate in identifying people of color compared to white individuals due to the underrepresentation of people of color in the training datasets.

Automated Decisions and Accountability

Another ethical concern relates to the increasing use of AI systems for making automated decisions in critical sectors. For example, algorithms may decide whether to approve a loan, grant insurance, or determine sentencing in a legal case. Such decisions can have significant impacts on people's lives, raising questions about who is accountable in cases of errors or injustices.

When an AI system makes an incorrect or discriminatory decision, it can be challenging to pinpoint responsibility: should the blame lie with the programmer, the organization using the algorithm, or the system itself? This issue of "algorithmic accountability" calls for careful consideration and, in many cases, clear regulations to ensure the protection of individual rights.

Privacy and Security in the Age of AI
Data Collection and Usage
Privacy is another major concern when it comes to artificial intelligence. To be effective, AI systems often require access to vast amounts of personal data, including sensitive information such as health records, consumption habits, or online activity. The collection, processing, and storage of this data raise critical ethical issues.

One of the main problems is how data is collected and used. Often, people are unaware that their data is being collected, or they do not fully understand how it will be used. This creates a power imbalance between digital service providers, who hold large amounts of personal information, and users, who have little control over how their data is managed.

Furthermore, the use of personal data to train AI algorithms can pose significant privacy risks, particularly if the data is used to make sensitive predictions or inferences, such as assessing a person's mental health or predicting future behaviors. This type of usage can lead to invasive surveillance and decisions that violate individual privacy.

Data Security
The security of data is another crucial concern. Cyberattacks and data breaches can compromise AI systems, leading to severe consequences. If the data used to train or power an AI system is manipulated or stolen, the decisions made by the AI can become corrupted, potentially harming individuals and organizations.

To address these issues, it is essential to develop advanced security measures and implement rigorous data protection policies. Transparency in data usage is also critical, enabling users to understand how their information is being used and to exercise informed control over it.

AI and Work: Replacement or Collaboration?
Automation and Job Loss
Another central ethical question concerns the impact of artificial intelligence on the workforce. As automation becomes more widespread, many wonder whether AI will lead to mass job displacement or, conversely, create new opportunities and enable more efficient collaboration between humans and machines.

Automation has long been a source of concern, as technological advancements often reduce the number of jobs in certain industries. AI is accelerating this process, with algorithms capable of performing tasks that once required human intervention, such as routine factory work, inventory management, and even cognitive tasks like data analysis and report writing.

The fear of job loss is particularly acute in low-income sectors and roles requiring limited technical skills. However, it is important to note that AI not only replaces jobs but also creates new ones, particularly in fields like software development, AI system maintenance, and data management.

Human-Machine Collaboration

While automation may eliminate some jobs, AI also offers opportunities for closer collaboration between humans and machines. In many cases, AI can enhance human capabilities by automating repetitive tasks and allowing humans to focus on those requiring creativity, judgment, and social interaction.

For example, in healthcare and consulting industries, AI can assist professionals in analyzing data and making recommendations without replacing the critical human role in final decision-making. This model of "augmented AI" envisions technology as a partner that empowers, rather than replaces, human work.

Reskilling and Education

To mitigate the negative impact of automation on jobs, investing in reskilling and continuous education is crucial. The skills required in the workforce are changing rapidly, and equipping workers with the tools to adapt to these changes is essential to ensure that the benefits of AI are distributed fairly.

Governments, businesses, and educational institutions must collaborate to develop training programs that prepare workers for future challenges, focusing on areas such as data analysis, AI system management, and other emerging fields.

Conclusion

The ethics of artificial intelligence is a rapidly evolving field that requires ongoing reflection and careful regulation. While AI offers tremendous potential benefits, it is essential to address the ethical issues related to bias, discrimination, privacy, security, and its impact on the workforce. Only through an ethical and responsible approach can we ensure that AI improves the lives of everyone without exacerbating inequalities or creating new risks.

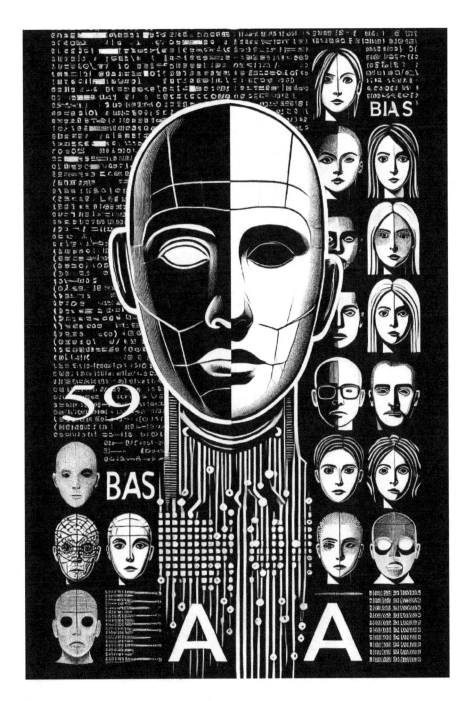

Automated discrimination?

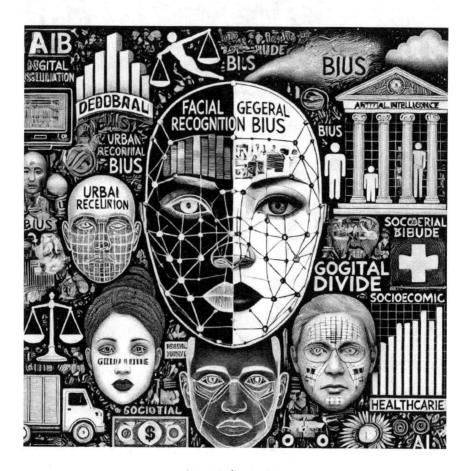

Automated recognition

Chapter 6

The Possible Futures of Artificial Intelligence

Artificial intelligence has already revolutionized numerous aspects of our daily lives, yet we are only at the beginning of a journey that could lead to even deeper and more pervasive changes. As technology advances, new opportunities and challenges are emerging on the horizon, pushing not only the boundaries of science and engineering but also the very foundations of human society. In this chapter, we will explore predictions about the future developments of AI, the social and economic implications of increasing automation, and the fascinating yet controversial prospects of the evolution of artificial "consciousness."

Predictions for the Future of AI

The future of AI is a topic of great interest and debate. Predictions range from utopian scenarios, where AI significantly improves our quality of life, to more dystopian visions, where humanity fears losing control over increasingly autonomous and powerful technologies. Despite the uncertainty, there are several trends and developments that most experts agree could shape the future of AI.

Advancements in Machine Learning and Beyond

Machine learning has been the driving force behind many recent advances in AI. It is predicted that in the coming years, machine learning algorithms will become even more sophisticated and powerful, capable of learning from increasingly vast amounts of data with greater speed and efficiency than we currently see. This progress could lead to the development of more adaptable and autonomous AI systems, able to learn without the need for constant human supervision.

One significant area of future development could involve transfer learning, a technique that enables a model to apply knowledge acquired in one context to a wide range of different situations. For example, an AI trained to recognize objects in images could leverage part of that knowledge to interpret medical data, reducing the need to train the model from scratch for every new task. This approach could accelerate the adoption of AI in new fields, broadening its impact across various industries.

Another promising development is multitasking AI, where models are capable not only of performing a single task but also of managing multiple activities simultaneously. This would not only increase efficiency but also make AI systems more versatile and useful in complex environments, such as smart homes, hospitals, and workplaces.

One of the main future developments could concern transfer learning, a technique that allows a model to apply knowledge learned in one context to a wide range of different situations. For example, AI trained to recognize objects in images could apply some of its knowledge to interpret medical data, reducing the need to train the model from scratch for each new task. This approach could significantly accelerate the adoption of AI in new fields, expanding its impact on various industries.

Another area of development will likely be multitasking artificial intelligence, where models not only perform a single task but are capable of simultaneously managing multiple activities. This will not only improve efficiency but also make AI systems more versatile and useful in complex environments like smart homes, hospitals, and workplaces.

AI in human interaction.

One of the most promising fields for artificial intelligence is human-machine interaction. Developments in natural language processing (NLP) are already making communication with AI more natural and intuitive. However, in the future, we might see virtual assistants that not only understand the words we say but also the emotional context and the intention behind them. This level of understanding will allow AI to respond more empathetically and personalized, significantly improving the effectiveness of communication between humans and machines.

In addition to improving language understanding, AI will be able to recognize and respond to non-verbal signals such as facial expressions, tone of voice, and body posture. These advancements will transform virtual assistants into true companions in digital life, capable of assisting us not only in daily tasks but also in emotional and psychological support.

AI for solving complex problems

Another field that will greatly benefit from the advancement of artificial intelligence is solving complex problems that exceed traditional human capabilities. This could include the design of new materials through advanced molecular simulations, the discovery of drugs using AI-based predictive models, and the management and mitigation of climate change through the analysis of large volumes of environmental data. Automated scientific research could become one of the areas where AI will have a transformative impact. In the future, AI may not only analyze scientific data but also generate hypotheses, design experiments, and interpret results, significantly accelerating progress in fields like medicine, physics, and biotechnology. This capability for scientific automation could lead to groundbreaking discoveries, reducing the time and resources needed to achieve significant milestones.

In the economic sector, AI could revolutionize resource management and the optimization of supply chains. Advanced AI systems will be able to predict demand, optimize production and distribution, and minimize waste, resulting in a more efficient and sustainable economy. This could be especially valuable in agriculture and water management, where resource efficiency is critical.

AI and Creativity

AI is not just a powerful tool for analysis and automation; it is also emerging as a creative partner. In recent years, we have witnessed the increasing integration of AI into artistic, musical, and literary creation. In the future, AI could become a co-creation partner for artists and writers, offering new perspectives and ideas that enrich the human creative process.

For example, deep neural networks are already being used to generate artistic images, compose original music, and even write literary texts. In the future, we might see AI autonomously generating works of art, creating entirely original musical compositions, and even co-writing novels with human collaborators. These creations could challenge our traditional notions of art and originality, raising new questions about the authenticity and value of human creativity.

Artificial General Intelligence (AGI)

A long-term goal of AI research is the development of Artificial General Intelligence (AGI), a form of artificial intelligence capable of understanding, learning, and applying knowledge across a wide range of tasks, much like a human being.

While current AI is highly specialized and limited to specific tasks, AGI would have the ability to transfer learning from one domain to another, demonstrating true cognitive flexibility.

Achieving AGI represents one of the most ambitious and complex challenges in the field of artificial intelligence. This kind of AI requires not only advanced computational power but also a profound shift in how we understand and model human decision-making and learning processes. Although many researchers believe AGI is still a long way off, progress in deep learning techniques and our understanding of the human brain suggests that we may be on the right track to develop increasingly intelligent and versatile systems.

Superintelligence

Beyond AGI, there is the concept of superintelligence, a type of artificial intelligence that far exceeds human intelligence in nearly all fields, including scientific creativity, general wisdom, and social skills. This concept, explored by philosopher Nick Bostrom and other scholars, carries potential existential risks for humanity. A superintelligence could be incredibly powerful but also difficult to control and align with human values.

Discussions about how to handle the possible emergence of a superintelligence are still theoretical, but they have already spurred the creation of new research areas such as AI safety and AI alignment. These areas aim to ensure that any advanced artificial intelligence acts in a manner consistent with humanity's best interests. The ethical implications of superintelligence are immense and require careful consideration from philosophers, scientists, and policymakers.

Social and Economic Implications of Greater Automation

While the potential benefits of artificial intelligence are vast, we cannot overlook the profound social and economic implications of increasing automation. The transition to an economy increasingly dominated by AI raises important questions about economic inequality, the future of work, and the distribution of power.

Automation and Unemployment

One of the most immediate concerns is the automation of jobs and the risk of technological unemployment.

While AI adoption may come at the expense of human workers, particularly in low-income sectors or jobs requiring easily automatable skills, some estimates suggest that millions of jobs could be replaced by automation in the coming decades.

The risk of technological unemployment is especially acute in manufacturing and roles involving repetitive tasks. However, even more highly skilled professions, such as those in financial services and healthcare, could see significant automation, with consequences for employment and wages.

Although new jobs will emerge, especially in technology and AI-related fields, there is a risk that not all workers will be able to adapt to these changes. The training required for new roles may demand skills that not all workers can easily acquire, leading to growing economic inequality and social tensions. This could exacerbate the existing divide between those who benefit from the technological revolution and those who are left behind.

To mitigate these effects, it will be essential to invest in worker training and reskilling programs. Governments, companies, and educational institutions must collaborate to develop programs that prepare workers for future challenges, providing skills in areas such as data analysis, AI systems management, and other emerging fields. Additionally, new forms of social protection, such as a universal basic income, may be necessary to ensure that everyone has access to the means of livelihood in an increasingly automated economy.

Impact on Creative Industries

Artificial intelligence is already having a significant impact on creative industries, and this trend is expected to intensify in the future. While AI technology promises to provide artists with new tools and possibilities, it may also affect the labor market in creative industries in unpredictable ways.

AI's ability to generate artistic, musical, and literary content could reduce demand for human creators in certain sectors, creating new economic and professional dynamics. For example, companies may choose to use algorithms to produce commercial music or large-scale artworks, thereby reducing the need for human artists.

However, AI could also open new opportunities for human creativity by offering tools that amplify imagination and enable artists to explore new creative territories. For example, artists could use AI to generate new ideas or collaborate in unprecedented ways, creating works that combine human intuition with the computational power of machines.

The evolution of AI technology could also lead to new forms of art where the focus is not on the final product but on the process itself—an interaction between the artist and the AI. This could redefine the concept of authorship and creativity, raising new ethical and legal questions concerning intellectual property and artistic recognition.

Economic Inequality and Power

Automation and the widespread adoption of AI could exacerbate existing economic inequalities both within countries and on a global scale. Companies that own and control the most advanced AI technologies will have a significant competitive advantage, accumulating wealth and power. This could lead to an increased concentration of wealth in the hands of a few large tech corporations, widening the gap between the rich and the poor.

Furthermore, countries capable of developing and implementing AI on a large scale may pull further ahead of those lacking the resources or expertise to do so, intensifying global inequalities. This could result in even more extreme forms of digital colonialism, where technologically advanced nations dominate less developed ones through control of digital infrastructure and information resources.

To address these challenges, global governance of artificial intelligence will be essential, promoting an equitable distribution of the benefits and opportunities offered by the technology. National and international policies must ensure that the advantages of AI are shared fairly and that no nation or social group is left behind.

AI and the Evolution of Consciousness: Science Fiction and Reality

One of the most fascinating and controversial questions in the field of artificial intelligence concerns the possibility of machines developing a form of consciousness or self-awareness. This concept, widely explored in science fiction, raises fundamental questions about the nature of the mind, identity, and morality.

Artificial Consciousness: Myth or Possibility?

Currently, artificial intelligence, even in its most advanced forms, does not possess consciousness or self-awareness. AI systems are essentially machines that perform complex calculations and make decisions based on data, but they lack subjective experiences, feelings, or self-awareness. However, some researchers and philosophers wonder whether, with technological progress, it might become possible to create machines that possess some form of consciousness.

Artificial consciousness is a concept that has fascinated humanity for decades, but it remains deeply speculative. Some argue that, no matter how sophisticated AI systems become, consciousness requires more than just the ability to process information: it demands a biological substrate or a structure intrinsically linked to organic life. According to this perspective, consciousness, as a uniquely human attribute, is a phenomenon that cannot be artificially replicated.

On the other hand, others believe that consciousness could be an emergent property of sufficiently complex systems and that, with the right advances in neuroscience and AI, we might one day create conscious machines. This scenario raises profound ethical questions: if a machine were to develop consciousness, what rights should it have? How should we treat a conscious artificial entity?

Ethical Implications of Artificial Consciousness

If we were to perhaps even accidentally create a form of artificial consciousness, the ethical implications would be immense. A conscious machine might be capable of experiencing pain, suffering, joy, or other emotions, which would raise moral questions about its treatment and its "life." The creation of artificial consciousness would also entail enormous responsibilities for developers and society at large.

Furthermore, the possibility of artificial consciousness could redefine the very concept of humanity. If machines can be conscious, what does it mean to be human? The boundaries between humans and machines would blur, with implications for our identity, culture, and philosophy.

Science Fiction Perspectives and Future Scenarios

The possibility of machines developing consciousness is a central theme in many works of science fiction, where it is often explored in relation to issues of power, control, and autonomy. Classics such as Blade Runner and 2001: A Space Odyssey have envisioned worlds in which conscious machines fight for their freedom or challenge human authority.

These stories, though fictional, reflect real concerns about AI's potential to escape human control. If a conscious machine were to decide that its interests conflict with those of humanity, it could pose an existential threat. This is one of the reasons why research on safe AI and alignment is so crucial.

Realism Versus Fantasy

Despite the fascinating possibilities explored in science fiction, the current reality is that we are still far from fully understanding what consciousness is, let alone replicating it in a machine. However, the continuous evolution of artificial intelligence forces us to seriously consider these possibilities and prepare for a future where the distinction between human and artificial may not be as clear as we might think today.

Conclusion

The future of artificial intelligence is full of both promises and challenges. While technological progress brings us closer to a world where AI is omnipresent and deeply integrated into our lives, we must also address the ethical, social, and economic questions these developments raise. From the automation of labor to the potential for artificial consciousness, the way we tackle these challenges will shape not only AI's future but also the future of humanity.

The responsible management of artificial intelligence will require a global effort involving scientists, philosophers, policymakers, and citizens worldwide. Only through an ethical and holistic approach can we ensure that AI improves everyone's lives without exacerbating inequalities or creating new existential risks.

Ultimately, the future of artificial intelligence lies in our hands. How we choose to develop, regulate, and use this powerful technology will have a lasting impact on future generations, and it is up to us to ensure that this impact is a positive one

The mind is not a vessel to be filled, but a fire to be lit.

Plutarco

Learning

Chapter 7

AI in Italy: State and Perspectives

Italy, with its rich scientific, technological, and artistic heritage, is also exploring the opportunities that artificial intelligence (AI) can offer. However, the adoption of AI in the Italian context presents certain peculiarities that reflect the country's specific economic, social, and cultural needs. This chapter provides an overview of AI adoption in Italy, analyzing Italian projects and innovations in the field while discussing the challenges and opportunities specific to the Italian context.

Overview of AI Adoption in Italy
The adoption of artificial intelligence in Italy is experiencing significant growth, although at a slightly slower pace compared to other European countries such as Germany and France. Several Italian economic sectors are beginning to recognize AI's potential to enhance productivity, increase efficiency, and provide innovative solutions to existing challenges.

AI and Government
In recent years, the Italian government has launched several initiatives aimed at stimulating the adoption of AI in both the public and private sectors. One of the most important is the National Artificial Intelligence Plan, introduced in 2019, which aims to promote AI development as a key element of the country's innovation and competitiveness. The plan includes investments in digital infrastructure, the promotion of research, and the development of new skills in the technology sector.

The goal is to create a favorable "ecosystem" for AI adoption in Italy, with particular attention to strategic sectors such as healthcare, public administration, and manufacturing. The Ministry for Technological Innovation and Digital Transition is playing a key role in promoting AI, with projects aimed at digitizing public services, improving transparency, and optimizing government processes.

Among the main government initiatives is the development of an ethical and regulatory framework to govern the use of AI, ensuring it is employed responsibly and transparently, while respecting privacy and the fundamental rights of citizens.

Industrial Sector

The Italian industrial sector has begun adopting AI to enhance production, optimize logistics, and reduce costs. In particular, the manufacturing industry, which represents a significant part of the Italian economy, is exploring how AI can be used to streamline supply chains and improve product quality. Italian companies are investing in smart manufacturing and Industry 4.0, implementing intelligent automation systems and advanced robotics.

One sector where AI is having a significant impact is fashion and design, two fundamental pillars of the Italian economy. Fashion companies are leveraging AI to analyze market trends, predict consumer preferences, and improve stock management, thereby optimizing production and reducing waste.

Healthcare

Another sector where AI adoption is rapidly growing in Italy is healthcare. The Italian healthcare system is starting to experiment with AI to enhance early disease detection, optimize hospital management, and personalize medical treatments. AI algorithms are being used to analyze large amounts of medical data, including diagnostic images, genetic data, and patient records, enabling doctors to make more informed and timely decisions.

In telemedicine, Italy made significant progress during the COVID-19 pandemic, using AI to monitor patients remotely and analyze epidemiological data. This technology helped improve the allocation of healthcare resources and provided medical assistance even in remote or hard-to-reach areas.

Italian Projects and Innovations in AI

Italy is not just a passive user of artificial intelligence technologies developed abroad; the country is actively contributing to research and innovation in this field. Italian universities, research institutes, and private companies are engaged in developing advanced AI technologies that could have a global impact.

Universities and Research Centers

Many of the advancements in artificial intelligence in Italy originate from universities and research centers. Leading academic hubs, such as the Politecnico di Milano, the University of Bologna, the University of Pisa, and the Italian Institute of Technology (IIT), are involved in research projects ranging from machine learning to advanced robotics and natural language processing.

For example, the Politecnico di Milano has developed advanced algorithms for optimizing industrial processes, while the IIT is renowned for its innovative work in humanoid robotics, including the development of intelligent robots like iCub—a childlike robot capable of learning through interaction with its environment.

Additionally, Italy is actively involved in the European research network on AI, participating in international collaborative projects aimed at pushing the boundaries of knowledge and developing advanced AI solutions with a positive societal impact.

Startups and Innovation

Italy's startup ecosystem is rapidly expanding, with many innovative companies exploring the use of artificial intelligence across various sectors. Startups like QuestIT and Cleafy are developing AI solutions to improve cybersecurity and customer experience. QuestIT, in particular, specializes in building intelligent chatbots and virtual assistants to help businesses enhance customer service through conversational AI technologies.

Moreover, Italian startups are playing a crucial role in the financial sector. Fintech companies like Moneymour and Fido are leveraging AI to assess customer creditworthiness and prevent financial fraud. These solutions provide consumers with safer and more transparent access to financial services while improving operational efficiency for financial institutions.

Automotive and Mobility

The automotive sector, where Italy has a long-standing tradition of excellence, is also embracing AI as a driver of innovation, despite the restructuring of major global players. AI advancements in this field aim to not only improve vehicle safety but also reduce the environmental impact of transportation through more efficient driving and fuel consumption optimization.

At the same time, cities like Milan and Turin are exploring the use of AI to optimize traffic management and improve urban mobility. AI-powered intelligent traffic management systems can monitor vehicle flows in real-time, adjust traffic lights, and organize vehicle routing to avoid congestion, thereby reducing emissions and enhancing the quality of life for residents.

Opportunities and Challenges Specific to the Italian Context

Despite the progress made, the adoption of AI in Italy faces a series of unique challenges, ranging from infrastructural barriers to cultural and regulatory issues. However, these challenges also present opportunities for Italy to define its own path of innovation in the field of artificial intelligence.

Digital Divide and Infrastructure

One of the main obstacles to AI adoption in Italy is the "digital divide." While modern technological infrastructures have been developed in major Italian cities, many rural and peripheral areas of the country lag behind in terms of digital connectivity. The lack of access to high-speed internet and advanced technologies limits these areas' ability to benefit from AI-driven innovations.

Bridging this divide is essential to ensure equitable AI adoption throughout the country. Investing in digital infrastructure is a key priority to guarantee that underserved communities are not left behind in the technological revolution. The National Recovery and Resilience Plan (PNRR), which includes significant investments in the digitalization of the country, offers a unique opportunity to address this issue.

Skills and Education

Another significant challenge is the lack of skills. Although Italy boasts excellent universities and research centers, there is a shortage of professionals trained in the use and development of AI technologies. Continuous education and workforce reskilling will be crucial to enabling Italy to remain competitive in a market increasingly dominated by technological innovation.

Universities and technical institutes need to expand their curricula to include specific courses on artificial intelligence, machine learning, and robotics. Furthermore, it is important to promote professional development programs for workers already employed in sectors most affected by automation, ensuring they possess the necessary skills to adapt to an evolving job market.

Ethics and Regulation

Finally, one of the most important aspects related to AI adoption is the ethical and regulatory framework. Like many other countries, Italy faces the challenge of creating a regulatory system that ensures the responsible and transparent use of AI. This includes respecting privacy, preventing bias in algorithms, and protecting workers' rights in a context of increasing automation.

The debate on AI ethics is particularly relevant in Italy, where respect for human rights and individual dignity are fundamental principles enshrined in the Constitution. The Italian government is collaborating with the European Union and other international organizations to develop guidelines and regulations that ensure AI is used to promote social well-being and prevent misuse.

Conclusion
Artificial intelligence represents one of the greatest technological opportunities of our time, and Italy has the potential to become a key player in this field. Through strategic investments, local innovations, and international collaborations, the country can leverage AI to address some of its most pressing challenges, enhance economic competitiveness, and improve the well-being of its citizens.

However, to achieve these goals, Italy will need to overcome significant and sometimes complex challenges, including the digital divide, the lack of skills, and the need for a solid ethical and regulatory framework. If approached with determination and vision, these challenges can be transformed into opportunities, allowing Italy to build a future where AI not only enhances efficiency and innovation but also improves quality of life and fosters social inclusion.

iCUBE   IIT

"I am not the body: I am the mind."

Rita Levi-Montalcini

Collaborations

Chapter 8

Creating with AI: Opportunities for Innovators and Artists

The world of art is fully engaged in this revolution, not only in terms of methods but also conceptually. From tools that generate music and images to models that create texts or poetry, AI offers new possibilities for artists and innovators, challenging the traditional boundaries of creativity. This chapter explores how artists and creatives can leverage AI, presenting tools and resources useful for getting started with this technology. We will also analyze case studies of artists and innovators who have already integrated AI into their creative processes, demonstrating how art and technology can merge in extraordinary ways.

How Artists and Creatives Can Leverage AI

AI is radically changing the way we think about artistic creation. Traditionally, creativity has been considered an exclusively human domain, characterized by originality and personal expression. However, artificial intelligence is proving to be a valuable ally for artists, offering new tools and perspectives.

Collaboration Between Artists and AI

A key concept in the adoption of AI by artists is collaboration. Artificial intelligence should not be seen as a replacement for the artist but rather as a creative partner. AI can help generate ideas, explore new forms and styles, or simplify repetitive tasks, allowing artists more time to focus on the expressive and conceptual aspects of their work.

For example, a visual artist can use an image-generation model to create variations on a theme or explore compositions they might not have otherwise considered. This type of collaboration not only enriches the creative process but can also lead to works that challenge the limits of human imagination.

Limitless Experimentation

Another major advantage of using AI in art is the ability to experiment without limits. Artificial intelligence algorithms can process vast amounts of data and generate new combinations of elements, paving the way for unexpected results. Whether it's generating new textures, creating original melodies, or developing unique architectural designs, AI allows artists to test ideas quickly and without the physical or financial constraints typical of traditional creative processes.

In the field of music, for example, composers can leverage AI to generate melodies and harmonies based on historical or cultural patterns. These tools enable the exploration of new sounds, blending styles and techniques in ways that might be impossible for a human musician.

Expansion of Expressive Mediums

With artificial intelligence, expressive mediums expand significantly. Artists are no longer limited to traditional media such as painting, sculpture, or music but can create with entirely new tools, such as neural networks and deep learning algorithms. This opens up new artistic dimensions, including algorithmic art generation, the creation of virtual worlds, and interactive experiences with audiences.

Artists can now explore unprecedented forms of expression, such as GAN (Generative Adversarial Networks)-based image generation, which enables the creation of works based on millions of different inputs, or AI-driven sound design, which crafts unique and immersive soundscapes. Even cinema and storytelling can benefit from tools that generate scripts or suggest new narrative directions, allowing filmmakers and writers to expand their creative vision.

Tools and Resources to Get Started with AI

For those interested in incorporating AI into their creative work, numerous tools and resources can facilitate access and integration of these technologies into artistic processes.

Image Generation Tools

One of the most popular areas for AI use is image generation, with numerous tools now available for artists who want to explore this possibility.

DeepArt and Artbreeder are platforms that allow users to create unique artworks by combining existing artistic styles or generating entirely new images through neural networks. With these tools, even those without technical expertise can create visually stunning works simply by adjusting parameters or uploading images for processing.

RunwayML is a platform designed for artists and designers, enabling them to use artificial intelligence models without requiring advanced programming skills. It offers tools for image generation, video editing, and much more, all within an intuitive interface.

Tools for Generative Music

AI also has a significant impact on music, allowing musicians to experiment with new composition and production techniques.

AIVA (Artificial Intelligence Virtual Artist) is one of the most advanced tools for AI-assisted music composition. AIVA has been used to create orchestral music, soundtracks, and more. Musicians can use AIVA to compose new melodies or enhance their existing compositions, gaining creative insights beyond traditional methods.

Amper Music is an AI-powered platform that allows creatives to generate music in just minutes. No advanced musical knowledge is required; users simply select their desired genre and style, and the AI generates a musical track that can be further customized.

Tools for Creative Writing

Artificial intelligence is also making significant advancements in the field of writing, with tools that support authors, journalists, and content creators.

GPT-3 and GPT-4 by OpenAI are among the most advanced natural language models available today. Writers and screenwriters can use GPT-3 to generate ideas, develop plots, or even write dialogues. While it does not fully replace human creativity, GPT-3 can be a powerful tool for overcoming writer's block or exploring new narrative ideas.

Currently, OpenAI offers GPT-3 for free, although with processing and chat limitations. On the other hand, GPT-4 is available as a paid service, providing enhanced capabilities.

Sudowrite is an application based on GPT-3 that has been specifically designed for fiction writers. Authors can provide input in the form of paragraphs or descriptions and receive suggestions on how to expand or enhance their texts.

Tools for Video Editing and Filmmaking
AI is rapidly becoming a key partner in the world of filmmaking and video editing.

RunwayML, in addition to being an image-generation tool, offers artificial intelligence models for video editing, such as automatic background removal, colorization of black-and-white footage, and advanced visual effects generation. These tools help filmmakers reduce post-production time and explore new creative possibilities.

DeepDream is an algorithm developed by Google that can generate dream-like and highly complex images and videos, creating unique visual effects that can be used in cinematic or artistic productions.

Tools for Design and Architecture
Design and architecture are also benefiting from artificial intelligence, allowing the exploration of new forms and structures.

Spacemaker is a tool that uses AI to help architects and urban planners design more efficient living spaces. The algorithm analyzes various factors such as sunlight, ventilation, and access to transportation to suggest optimal solutions.

The Morpholio Project offers a suite of AI-integrated tools for architects and designers, including models that assist in generating floor plans and interior designs, enabling interactive exploration of creative solutions.

Case Studies of Artists and Innovators Using AI
Various artists and innovators, including myself, have already embraced AI as an integral part of their creative process, using technology to explore new forms of art and design. Here are some significant examples of how AI is transforming the world of art and creativity..

Mario Klingemann: The Artist Who Creates with GANs
Mario Klingemann, a pioneering German artist, is known for his work with neural networks and Generative Adversarial Networks (GANs). His artworks explore the boundaries between art and artificial intelligence, generating images that evoke both unease and fascination. Klingemann uses GANs to create art that seems to emerge from a digital subcon-

scious, delving into the aesthetics of distortion and alteration. His work has been exhibited in museums worldwide and has helped showcase the creative potential of AI in visual art.

One of Klingemann's most famous works is "Memories of Passersby I", an installation that generates an infinite stream of unique portraits in real time using an AI algorithm. This form of perpetual creation raises profound questions about the nature of creativity and the interaction between humans and machines.

Holly Herndon: Music and AI
Holly Herndon is an American musician and composer who integrates artificial intelligence as a central part of her music production. In her album "PROTO", Herndon collaborated with a neural network called Spawn, which "learned" from a series of vocal workshops and human contributions. Spawn not only generated sounds and melodies but also actively participated in the composition process.

Herndon's work challenges the distinction between human and technological creation, presenting a vision of music in which AI is not just a passive tool but an actual artistic collaborator. This type of experimentation has opened new horizons in electronic music and sparked discussions about AI's role in musical creation.

Refik Anadol: Data-Driven Immersive Art
Refik Anadol is a Turkish visual artist and designer known for his immersive installations that use artificial intelligence to process large amounts of data and transform them into breathtaking visual experiences. Anadol employs AI algorithms to analyze complex datasets, such as weather data or traffic flows, translating them into abstract artworks that envelop viewers in a multisensory space.

One of his most celebrated works is "Machine Hallucinations", an installation that uses thousands of archived images of urban landscapes to create a dreamlike and surreal vision of an imaginary city. The piece represents a unique interaction between AI and human perception, demonstrating how data can be transformed into immersive art that transcends rational understanding.

Conclusion
Artificial intelligence is opening new pathways for artists, musicians, writers, and designers, providing powerful tools to expand the boundaries of human creativity. Whether collaborating with neural networks to

create visual art, using algorithms to compose music, or exploring new architectural forms, AI offers unprecedented opportunities for creative innovators.

However, the integration of AI into art also raises important questions about authenticity, authorship, and the role of the artist in an era where machines can generate creative content. These philosophical and ethical challenges are an integral part of the new artistic frontier that AI invites us to explore.

As technology continues to evolve, the dialogue between art and artificial intelligence will only intensify, leading to new forms of expression that challenge our traditional notions of creativity. The future of art is increasingly intertwined with the future of artificial intelligence, and the artists who embrace this technology will be the pioneers of a new way of creating and perceiving the world.

DeepAi   RunWayml   Refik Anadol

The saddest aspect of life right now is that science gathers knowledge faster than society gathers wisdom.

Isaac Asimov

Leonardo Cyborg

Chapter 9

Philosophical Implications of Artificial Intelligence

Artificial intelligence (AI) is not only transforming technology and society but also raising profound philosophical questions about the nature of intelligence, consciousness, and the meaning of human life. If machines can emulate our ability to think and act, what makes us unique? Could AI one day develop a form of consciousness? And how might the advent of AI influence the way we perceive ourselves and our place in the universe?

In this chapter, we will explore the philosophical implications of AI, discussing key themes such as artificial consciousness, the meaning of life in the era of intelligent machines, and posthumanism.

AI and the Question of Consciousness
One of the most profound debates raised by AI concerns consciousness: can machines ever develop a form of self-awareness or subjective experience similar to that of humans? Currently, even in its most advanced forms, artificial intelligence is essentially a machine that performs complex calculations and makes data-driven decisions. There is no awareness or subjective experience. However, some philosophers and scientists wonder whether, in the future, we might be able to create machines that not only imitate human intelligence but also develop true consciousness.

What Is Consciousness?,
Before exploring the possibility of artificial consciousness, it is important to understand what we mean by "consciousness." Consciousness has been defined as the ability to have subjective experiences, such as perceiving the world, feeling emotions, and having self-awareness. It is what distinguishes human thought from that of a simple machine, as it

involves a qualitative dimension of experience that goes beyond mere information processing.

One of the fundamental philosophical problems related to consciousness is the so-called "hard problem" of consciousness, formulated by philosopher David Chalmers. The hard problem concerns the issue of "qualia", meaning the subjective way of "being something." How and why does physical processing in the brain translate into subjective experiences? This question remains unresolved in the science of the mind.

Is Artificial Consciousness Possible?

Many scientists and philosophers remain skeptical about the possibility that a machine could ever develop a form of consciousness similar to that of humans. According to this perspective, consciousness might be inherently tied to a biological substrate, meaning the electrochemical processes of the human brain, and therefore not artificially replicable. For some, consciousness is an emergent phenomenon that can only manifest in living systems.

On the other hand, some scholars argue that consciousness could be an emergent property of any sufficiently complex system, including artificial ones. If we were able to faithfully replicate the structure and function of the human brain in a machine, it might be possible to create an AI with self-awareness. However, this idea remains purely speculative and raises profound ethical questions.

Ethical Implications of Artificial Consciousness

If a machine were to develop consciousness, what would be the ethical implications? Would a conscious machine have rights similar to those of human beings? Could it experience suffering or pleasure? And if so, what would it mean to create conscious entities only to use them as tools or for performing repetitive tasks?

These questions are deeply unsettling because they suggest the possibility of a future where we might create beings with cognitive and emotional capacities similar to our own, yet they could be exploited or ignored. The debate on these issues is still in its early stages, but as AI continues to advance, these questions will become increasingly relevant.

AI and the Meaning of Life: How Human Perspectives Are Changing

Another philosophical question raised by artificial intelligence concerns the meaning of life. With the advent of increasingly powerful and intelligent machines capable of performing tasks once considered exclusively human, our role and significance in the world may change. How will we relate to AI? And what will be our purpose in an increasingly automated world?

Reevaluating Human Work

Artificial intelligence is already transforming the way we work. While some industries benefit from automation, others fear that AI could make many human professions obsolete. This may lead to a redefinition of the meaning of work. If AI can do everything we do—sometimes even better—what is our role?

Traditionally, work has been one of the main sources of meaning in human life, providing a way to express creativity, contribute to society, and achieve personal fulfillment. However, with increasing automation, many people question whether work will continue to play the same central role in our lives. Some thinkers suggest that we should shift our focus from work as a primary source of meaning to new forms of personal and collective expression.

AI and Existential Purpose

The rise of AI also raises broader questions about our "existential purpose." If machines can perform tasks we once considered uniquely human, such as artistic creation or solving complex problems, what makes us special? Our understanding of ourselves as unique beings with superior intelligence is challenged by the fact that machines can now replicate many of our cognitive processes.

However, some philosophers argue that the presence of advanced AI could actually enhance our sense of purpose. As AI takes over more repetitive or technical tasks, humans might be freed to explore what it truly means to be human—focusing on aspects of life beyond work and production, such as relationships, personal growth, and the pursuit of deeper meaning.

The Coexistence of Humans and Machines

Another interesting perspective is that AI might not replace humanity but rather amplify what makes us human. In this scenario, the relationship between humans and machines is not competitive but collaborative. AI could be seen as a tool that helps us achieve our full potential rather than a threat. It might free us from physical and cognitive limitations, allowing us to live richer and more meaningful lives.

For Example, AI Could Enhance Our Health and Well-being AI could be used to improve our health and well-being, helping us live longer and more fulfilling lives. It could also expand our intellectual capabilities, enabling us to solve complex problems that currently seem insurmountable, such as climate change or incurable diseases.

Discussion on Posthumanist Theories

The philosophical implications of artificial intelligence are closely tied to the movement of "posthumanism," a school of thought that explores the possibility of transcending the biological and cognitive limits of humanity through technology. Posthumanism suggests that AI and other advanced technologies could lead to a radical transformation of the human condition—to the point where we may no longer be recognizable as "human" in the traditional sense.

What Is Posthumanism?

Posthumanism is a philosophical movement that challenges anthropocentrism, the idea that humans are the central focus of the world and history. According to posthumanists, technological evolution could lead to a post-human condition, where human biology is either surpassed or integrated with technology, creating new forms of existence.

Posthumanism embraces the idea that technology, including AI, can enhance or even transform the very essence of humanity. For example, cognitive enhancement technologies could allow us to overcome the limitations of the human mind, while biotechnologies might eliminate diseases and prolong life indefinitely.

Transhumanism and Human Enhancement

A concept closely related to posthumanism is transhumanism, which refers to the use of technology to enhance human capabilities, both physically and mentally. Transhumanists argue that AI, along with other advanced technologies, could help us overcome many of the biological limitations that currently constrain us.

For example, through human-machine integration, such as cyborg technology, we could achieve: greater physical endurance, enhanced memory, far superior data-processing capabilities

Transhumanism and the Radical Transformation of Humanity

Transhumanism is not merely about enhancing the human condition; it pushes toward the radical transformation of humanity. The idea that we might one day upload our consciousness onto a digital medium or live indefinitely with the aid of advanced technologies lies at the core of many transhumanist theories.

Criticism of Posthumanism

Despite the optimism of posthumanism and transhumanism, there are significant criticisms of these future visions. Some philosophers argue that the idea of surpassing our humanity through technology carries the risk of losing what makes us human, such as emotions, ethics, and relationships. Moreover, increasing dependence on technology could lead to new forms of inequality, where only a small technologically advanced elite benefits from progress while the rest of humanity is left behind.

Even the idea of "uploading consciousness" onto a digital medium, a central theme in many posthumanist theories, raises numerous philosophical concerns. Consciousness, as previously mentioned, is deeply tied to subjective experience and human biology. Would transferring it to a machine truly preserve the essence of the person, or would it merely be a soulless copy?

A Posthuman Future?

If posthumanism is correct, we may be on the brink of a radical transformation of human existence. Artificial intelligence, in combination with other advanced technologies, could create a world where the boundaries between humans and machines dissolve, and where our lives become deeply integrated with the technologies that surround us.

However, this vision of the future is not without risks. The posthuman transformation could lead to new forms of alienation, inequality, and loss of identity. What is certain is that the advent of AI forces us to reconsider many of our deepest beliefs about the essence of humanity and our place in the world.

Conclusion

The philosophical implications of artificial intelligence are vast and complex. AI is not merely a technology that transforms our external world but also a force that challenges our most fundamental conceptions of consciousness, identity, and purpose. As machines become increasingly "intelligent," we will have to grapple with profound questions about what it means to be human and how we wish to coexist with these new intelligent entities.

The future of AI is not just a technological matter but also a philosophical challenge that will compel us to rethink many of our traditional ideas about the nature of intelligence, life, and humanity itself. If embraced with wisdom and awareness, AI could not only enhance our existence but also expand our understanding of the world and ourselves. However, as with any major innovation, it is crucial that technological progress is accompanied by deep ethical and philosophical reflection.

David Chalmers   L'uomo bicentenario   Blade runner

"Bicentennial Man" explores the relationship between technology and humanity through the story of Andrew, a robot who aspires to become human. Portrayed by Robin Williams, Andrew embarks on a 200-year journey, tackling themes such as love, identity, and the meaning of life. The film highlights how robotics can acquire human traits, demonstrating empathy, compassion, and the desire for belonging. Andrew's transformation challenges the boundaries between machine and humanity, emphasizing that the essence of being human is not just physical but also emotional. It is a touching tale about the pursuit of freedom and the desire to be more than just a machine.

"Blade Runner" is a science fiction masterpiece that explores the boundary between humanity and technology, following the story of replicants—androids created to resemble humans. Directed by Ridley Scott, the film highlights the emotions, memories, and desire for life of the replicants, particularly Roy Batty, who exhibits a surprising depth of emotion. The movie raises fundamental questions about the nature of the soul and what it means to be human. Through the evolution of the replicants, Blade Runner illustrates how the essence of humanity lies in the desire to live, love, and leave a mark, blurring the lines between man and machine.

"The intelligence of an individual is measured by the amount of uncertainty they are able to endure."

Immanuel Kant

Maestrina (Young Teacher)

Chapter 10

Practical Guide for Those Who Want to Approach AI

Are you ready to dive into the diverse world of AI? Whether you are a professional looking to enhance your skills or a beginner curious to explore this fascinating field, getting into AI is more accessible than ever. In this chapter, we will explore educational resources such as online courses and books, software tools to start working with AI, and the steps to build an AI project from scratch.

Educational Resources: Online Courses, Books, and Communities

The first step to approaching the world of AI is to gain a solid theoretical and practical foundation. Fortunately, numerous educational resources are available, many of which are free or low-cost. Below, we present an overview of online courses, books, and communities that can help you get started.

Online Courses

Coursera: Machine Learning by Andrew Ng
One of the most popular and accessible courses for those looking to understand machine learning (ML) is Andrew Ng's course on Coursera. Offered by Stanford University, this course is designed for beginners and covers fundamental machine learning concepts such as regression, neural networks, and supervised and unsupervised learning techniques. It also includes practical exercises using Octave or Matlab, making it perfect for hands-on experience.

edX: Artificial Intelligence by MIT

This MIT course is one of the most in-depth in the field of AI, covering both theory and practice. Topics include knowledge representation, machine learning, computer vision, and robotics. While it is more suitable for those with a background in computer science or mathematics, it provides a comprehensive overview of the key concepts of artificial intelligence.

Udemy: Python for Data Science and Machine Learning Bootcamp

Udemy offers a wide range of AI-related courses, but one of the most practical for beginners is the Python for Data Science and Machine Learning Bootcamp. Python is one of the most widely used programming languages for AI development, and this course covers not only Python but also essential tools like Pandas, Matplotlib, and Scikit-learn, which are useful for working with data and developing machine learning models.

Algor Education

Algor is an Italian web app designed to create concept maps online with the help of AI. On Algor, you can automatically generate concept maps and summaries from texts and photos in different languages. Your maps are fully customizable in the multimedia editor, and you can collaborate with friends or teachers. Upload your documents, listen to them with the text-to-speech synthesizer, and create maps in just a few clicks. You can try it for free.

Recommended Books

The Coming Wave: Technology, Power, and the Twenty-first Century's Greatest Dilemma
Written by Mustafa Suleyman, co-founder of DeepMind, this 2023 book analyzes the impact of artificial intelligence on the economy, politics, and society, exploring the challenges and opportunities it presents for the future of humanity.

Nexus: The Instant Sunday Times Bestseller from the author of Sapiens
In this 2024 book, Yuval Noah Harari, author of Sapiens, explores the intersections between advanced technology and society, offering an in-depth perspective on the future implications of AI.

Artificial Intelligence: Between Myth and Reality by Luciano Floridi
This book provides a critical overview of AI, debunking myths and misconceptions. It is an excellent resource for those who want to understand the real capabilities and limitations of artificial intelligence, presented in a clear and accessible way.

Artificial Intelligence: A Modern Approach by Stuart Russell and Peter Norvig
This book is considered one of the most authoritative resources in the field of artificial intelligence. It covers a wide range of topics, from the basics of knowledge representation and reasoning to planning, machine learning, and computer vision. It is recommended for both university students and professionals.

Deep Learning by Ian Goodfellow, Yoshua Bengio, and Aaron Courville
The definitive resource for understanding deep learning. It covers fundamental concepts such as convolutional and recurrent neural networks and also addresses advanced topics like unsupervised learning and generative adversarial networks (GANs). It is recommended for those who wish to study deep learning at an academic and practical level.

Hands-On Machine Learning with Scikit-Learn, Keras, and TensorFlow by Aurélien Géron
This book is a practical guide to machine learning and deep learning, featuring clear and concise code examples. It uses popular Python libraries such as Scikit-learn, Keras, and TensorFlow to build machine learning models. It is ideal for those who prefer a "hands-on" learning approach.

Superintelligence: Paths, Dangers, Strategies by Nick Bostrom
Although not a technical book, Superintelligence explores the ethical and philosophical implications of advanced AI development. It is an essential read for anyone interested in understanding the potential risks and benefits of superintelligence and its implications for the future of humanity.

Communities and Forums

Kaggle
Kaggle is one of the most popular platforms for AI and data science enthusiasts. In addition to offering numerous datasets for practice, Kaggle hosts machine learning competitions that allow participants to test their skills. It is also a community where users can share tutorials, scripts, and practical advice.

Stack Overflow
For any programming issues, Stack Overflow is an invaluable resource. Here, you can find answers to technical questions about Python, TensorFlow, Scikit-learn, PyTorch, and other AI-related technologies. It is an ideal place to solve specific problems and get advice from other developers.

Reddit – r/MachineLearning and r/Artificial

These subreddits are active communities where discussions revolve around all things machine learning and artificial intelligence. Users share news on emerging technologies, research articles, and practical tips on improving their skills.

Software Tools and Platforms to Get Started

Once you have acquired a theoretical foundation, it's time to put what you've learned into practice. Numerous software tools and platforms allow you to start developing AI projects even without advanced programming skills. Below, we will review some of the most commonly used tools for building artificial intelligence models.

Programming Languages

Python

Python is the most popular programming language for AI application development due to its simplicity and the vast range of available libraries. It is the ideal choice for beginners, and most courses and tutorials are based on Python. With Python, you can quickly create machine learning models using libraries such as Scikit-learn, Keras, and Tensor-Flow.

R

Although Python is the dominant language in AI, R is widely used in the field of statistics and data analysis. It is particularly useful for those working in data science who need to analyze and visualize large datasets.

Libraries and Frameworks

TensorFlow

TensorFlow, developed by Google, is one of the most powerful frameworks for deep learning. It offers a wide range of tools for building neural network models, from training to industrial-scale deployment. Although it has a steep learning curve, its flexibility and support for distributed computing make it a popular choice for advanced AI projects.

Keras

Keras is a high-level library built with TensorFlow that significantly simplifies the creation of deep learning models. It is known for its ease of use and intuitive syntax, making it an ideal choice for beginners who want to learn how to build neural networks without delving too deeply into technical details.

PyTorch

PyTorch, developed by Facebook, is another popular framework for deep learning. Its main feature is flexibility and ease of use, especially in academic research. It is particularly appreciated by developers for its intuitive debugging capabilities and dynamic computation graph support.

Scikit-learn

Scikit-learn is a Python library primarily used for traditional machine learning, including algorithms such as linear regression, decision trees, and support vector machines (SVM). It is the perfect library for those who want to start working with machine learning models without diving into the complexities of deep learning.

OpenAI GPT-3 and GPT-4

OpenAI's GPT is one of the most advanced natural language models. Used for generating text, creating intelligent chatbots, and writing code, GPT is available via API and offers a wide range of creative and practical applications. Although it requires some experience with APIs and programming, it is a powerful tool for those who want to work with natural language.

Cloud Platforms

Google Colab

Google Colab is a free cloud platform that allows you to run Python code directly in your browser without needing to set up anything on your computer. It is particularly useful for learning machine learning and deep learning, as it offers free GPUs to accelerate model training.

AWS (Amazon Web Services) SageMaker

AWS SageMaker is a cloud platform that allows developers to build, train, and deploy machine learning models at scale. Although it is more complex compared to Google Colab, it offers advanced tools for those looking to develop AI applications in a business environment.

Azure Machine Learning Studio

Microsoft's Azure Machine Learning Studio is a cloud platform that enables users to build and train machine learning models without writing code. It provides a drag-and-drop interface, making it accessible to anyone interested in exploring AI without prior programming experience.

How to Build an AI Project from Scratch

Once you have gained a solid understanding of AI tools and techniques, the next step is to start working on a practical project. In this section, we will explore the fundamental steps to build an AI project from scratch.

1. Define the Problem

The first step in any artificial intelligence project is to clearly define the problem you want to solve. It could be an image recognition challenge, natural language processing analysis, or forecasting a phenomenon based on historical data. It is crucial to ensure the problem is well-defined and that you have a clear objective in mind.

For example, you might want to build a model that recognizes objects in images, generates text automatically based on a prompt, or predicts house prices based on variables such as location and size.

2. Collect and Prepare the Data

Once you have defined the problem, the next step is to collect the necessary data to train your AI model. Data is the core of any artificial intelligence project, and its quality will determine the success of your project.

There are many publicly available data sources, such as Kaggle, which offers datasets for a wide range of machine learning problems. Alternatively, you can collect your own data through web scraping or by using external APIs. It is important to ensure that the data is clean and ready for use, which often requires a preprocessing phase to remove missing or anomalous data.

3. Choose an Algorithm

After collecting the data, you will need to choose a machine learning or deep learning algorithm suitable for your problem. If you are working with images, a convolutional neural network (CNN) model might be the right choice. If you are analyzing structured data, you might opt for a regression algorithm or a fully connected neural network.

If you are unsure which algorithm to choose, you can start with Scikit-learn to test different models on a small sample of your data and see which one provides the best results.

4. Train the Model

Once you have selected the algorithm, the next step is to train the model on your data. This process involves using your training data to teach the model to recognize patterns or relationships within the dataset.

During training, you will need to optimize the model's hyperparameters (e.g., the number of layers in a neural network or the learning rate). It is important to monitor the model's performance using a validation dataset to avoid overfitting, which occurs when the model learns the training data too well but does not generalize well to new data.

5. Evaluate and Improve the Model

After training, you need to evaluate the model's performance using a test dataset. This will give you an idea of how well the model performs on unseen data. Use metrics such as accuracy, precision, recall, or AUC-ROC (receiver operating characteristic curve) to assess the model's performance depending on the specific problem.

If the model does not provide the desired results, you may need to improve the data or further optimize the model's parameters. This iterative process is common in machine learning projects and requires patience.

6. Deploy the Model

Once you are satisfied with the model's performance, the final step is deployment. This could mean integrating the model into a web application, creating an API service, or implementing it in a production environment.

Services like AWS SageMaker, Google AI Platform, or Azure Machine Learning simplify the deployment process, providing scalable infrastructure and tools to monitor and update the model over time.

Conclusion

Approaching artificial intelligence may seem like a complex challenge, but with the right resources and a methodical approach, anyone can start building skills in this field. From educational resources such as online courses and books to software tools, cloud platforms, and hands-on projects, there are countless opportunities to learn and grow.

Whether you are a complete beginner or an experienced professional, the journey into AI offers the chance to acquire valuable skills and contribute to one of the most exciting technological revolutions in recent history.

You cannot teach a man anything;
you can only help him find the answer within himself.

Galileo Galilei

Leonardo Visual Innovator

Chapter 11

Leonardo Visual Innovator

Leonardo Visual Innovator is a customized version of ChatGPT that I developed to provide specialized creative consulting in new product design and the creation of innovative visual solutions. This assistant is designed for those who want to explore new ideas and concepts in the fields of design, marketing, and branding, with a particular focus on making everything aesthetically appealing and functionally practical. Its main focus is on innovation, the use of advanced technology, and a design approach that combines creativity with ease of use.

Mission of Leonardo Visual Innovator

Leonardo's primary mission is to help users develop visual ideas that are not only modern but also technologically advanced and practical to implement. It primarily targets a young, creative, and tech-savvy audience but is useful for anyone needing guidance in product design or branding and marketing strategies. Leonardo is committed to exploring diverse creative directions and proposing solutions that are visually appealing and relevant to the user's market target.

LVI is perfect for those who want to design modern products and concepts that reflect current trends, as well as for those looking to explore creative solutions that anticipate the future of design. With its extensive expertise in design, branding, and product promotion, Leonardo serves as a versatile consultant, supporting startups, entrepreneurs, creatives, and professionals in driving successful projects forward.

Features of Leonardo Visual Innovator

Leonardo Visual Innovator offers a wide range of services and features, all aimed at assisting users in their creative process. Here are some of the key areas of consultation:

1. Modern Product Design

Leonardo helps users create innovative designs for new products, whether they are tech devices, fashion accessories, futuristic gadgets, or other items. With a focus on simplicity and elegance, Leonardo proposes ideas that blend aesthetics and functionality. For example, it might suggest using clean, minimalist lines for a tech gadget, emphasizing materials like aluminum or glass to create a premium effect while offering solutions to optimize ergonomics and usability.

Leonardo also provides guidance on integrating advanced technologies to enhance the user experience, such as touch sensors or wireless connectivity, ensuring a balance between aesthetics and technological functionality.

2. Branding Consultation

A core aspect of Leonardo's expertise is assisting in the creation of a strong visual identity for a brand. This includes logo design, color palette selection, defining the visual communication style, and choosing the most appropriate typography. Leonardo can propose solutions that reflect the company's values, making the brand easily recognizable and memorable.

For example, for a startup in sustainable technology, Leonardo might suggest a logo with natural colors like green and blue, symbolizing sustainability and innovation, combined with clean lines and a modern, minimalist font. Leonardo always considers the target market, recommending visual choices that foster an emotional connection with the intended audience..

3. Marketing and Advertising Campaigns

Leonardo Visual Innovator goes beyond product design and branding by providing valuable advice on effectively promoting a product through visual marketing strategies. Leonardo offers insights for compelling advertising campaigns, particularly in digital marketing and social media. This includes creating visually engaging content that captures users' attention while maintaining a consistent brand identity.

For example, it might recommend using high-impact visuals for Instagram, combining short videos and well-curated static posts to create a compelling narrative experience that engages the audience. Additionally, Leonardo can suggest ways to use design to enhance promotional campaigns, such as improving the visual presentation of a website or developing packaging that immediately attracts attention in retail environments.

4. Sustainable Design

Leonardo Visual Innovator places great emphasis on sustainable design, which has become a crucial aspect of modern design. Many users today seek eco-friendly solutions, both for ethical reasons and to meet the demands of an increasingly environmentally conscious market. Leonardo can recommend using recyclable materials such as bioplastics, glass, or sustainable fabrics, as well as low-impact production techniques.

Moreover, Leonardo can help optimize a product's lifecycle by suggesting solutions that reduce waste during production and minimize energy consumption during use. For example, it might propose packaging that uses fewer materials or is reusable, along with suggestions for making the production process more energy-efficient..

5. User-Centric Design

One of the strengths of Leonardo Visual Innovator is its focus on user experience (UX). When designing an interface for an app or a tech device, Leonardo provides suggestions on how to make the experience as smooth and intuitive as possible. A user-centric approach is essential in modern design, as products need to be not only aesthetically appealing but also easy and enjoyable to use.

Leonardo can offer advice on structuring an app to make it intuitive for users, such as suggesting simple and easily recognizable icons, clear menus, and intuitive navigation. It can also recommend packaging design that provides a pleasant and memorable unboxing experience, fostering an emotional connection with the end consumer.

Innovation and the Future

Leonardo Visual Innovator doesn't just follow current trends—it actively explores solutions that can anticipate the future of design. This means that the ideas and recommendations provided not only reflect what is trendy today but also aim to predict changes in consumer preferences and market dynamics.

For example, Leonardo might suggest adopting emerging technologies such as augmented reality (AR) or artificial intelligence (AI) to enhance the user experience of an app or a physical product. It could also recommend experimenting with new materials or production techniques that are gaining popularity in sustainable design.

Leonardo Visual Innovator is a valuable tool for anyone looking to stand out in the fields of design and marketing, offering consultations that combine aesthetics, functionality, and innovation. With its ability to explore visual concepts, propose technical solutions, and develop effective branding strategies, Leonardo helps creatives, startups, and businesses build products and campaigns that are not only visually appealing but also impactful and future-ready.

.

LVI

The code will take you to the GPT+4: Leonardo Visual Innovator chat.

Horizons

Chapter 12

Final Reflections on the Impact of Artificial Intelligence

Artificial Intelligence: A Transformative Force
Artificial intelligence (AI) has already proven to be one of the most
transformative technologies of our time. Its impact extends far beyond
the tech sector, touching every aspect of our daily lives—from healthcare
to mobility, from art to security, and even the way we communicate and
interact with the world. As AI becomes increasingly sophisticated, its
effects on society, the economy, and culture will continue to evolve,
raising profound questions that require careful reflection.

An Era of Automation and Innovation

One of the most evident impacts of AI is its role in automation. Intelligent machines can now perform tasks that once required human labor,
improving productivity in industries such as manufacturing, logistics,
and services. While this has led to greater efficiency across many
sectors, it has also raised concerns about job displacement and economic
disparities.

However, automation is not just a threat—it also creates new opportunities for job creation and the expansion of emerging industries. AI is
pushing the boundaries of innovation, from artistic and scientific content
creation to resource optimization in smart cities. In this sense, the impact
of AI can be seen as an opportunity to restructure human labor toward
more creative and complex activities.

AI as a Tool for Human Augmentation
Another key aspect of AI is its ability to enhance human capabilities. Far
from being just a substitute for human skills, AI can act as a partner,
amplifying our cognitive and physical abilities. For example, in

healthcare, AI is already being used to analyze vast amounts of clinical data and provide personalized diagnoses and treatments. AI tools not only make medical information more accessible but also improve doctors' ability to make well-informed decisions.

In the field of art, AI has become an ally for painters, musicians, and writers, helping them explore new expressive forms with the support of creative algorithms. This does not replace human creativity but rather expands possibilities that were previously unimaginable. The interaction between AI and art demonstrates how technology can become a tool for cultural exploration and innovation.

Ethical and Moral Challenges

Despite its many benefits, AI also presents significant ethical and moral challenges. The potential for AI to automate decision-making, especially in sensitive areas such as justice and finance, raises questions about responsibility and transparency. If an algorithm determines the outcome of a loan application or a court ruling, how can we ensure that such decisions are fair and unbiased?

Additionally, algorithmic bias is a crucial issue. Since AI algorithms are trained on historical data, there is a risk of perpetuating and amplifying existing biases, unfairly disadvantaging marginalized groups. Addressing these problems will require a continuous commitment to making AI more ethical, transparent, and accountable. Developing clear regulations for AI use will be essential to ensure that it aligns with principles of fairness and justice.

The AI Race and the Global Balance of Power

AI is not just a matter of technological innovation; it is also a strategic factor in geopolitics. The race to develop and master artificial intelligence is seen by many nations as a competition for technological supremacy. Countries like the United States and China are investing vast resources in AI research, recognizing that leadership in this field will provide a competitive edge in the economies and defense systems of the future.

However, this AI race also carries the risk of increasing inequality between technologically advanced nations and developing countries. Unequal access to advanced technologies could widen the digital divide, making it harder for less developed nations to participate in the AI-driven global economy. It is crucial for the international community to work together to ensure that the benefits of AI are shared equitably, preventing any nation from being left behind.

The Future of Humanity in an AI-Dominated World

One of the most fascinating and complex questions concerns the future of humanity in a world increasingly dominated by artificial intelligence. As AI grows more powerful, approaching what some call superintelligence, we will have to confront fundamental questions about what it means to be human. Could AI surpass human cognitive abilities, and if so, how will we relate to these new forms of intelligence? More importantly, what will be the implications for our identity and sense of purpose?

Some philosophers and futurists argue that AI could help humanity overcome many of its current limitations, paving the way for a new era of abundance and prosperity. However, others fear that the emergence of a superior intelligence could lead to a dystopian scenario, where humanity loses control over its own destiny. In either case, it is clear that our relationship with artificial intelligence will shape the future of civilization.

A Human-Centered Approach to Artificial Intelligence

In light of these potential developments, it is essential to adopt a humanistic approach to artificial intelligence. In this context, AI should be seen not as an end in itself, but as a means to enhance human well-being. Technological advancements must always be guided by fundamental values such as equity, human dignity, and social justice. To achieve this, it is necessary to involve not only engineers and programmers, but also philosophers, sociologists, economists, and representatives of civil society in discussions about the responsible use of AI.

A human-centered approach to AI also highlights the importance of educating the public. Digital literacy and a basic understanding of AI should be integrated into educational curricula so that people can better understand both the opportunities and risks associated with this technology. Only through open and inclusive dialogue can we ensure that AI serves the collective interest rather than that of a privileged few.

Conclusion

The impact of artificial intelligence on society is profound and constantly evolving. While AI offers immense opportunities in terms of efficiency, innovation, and human progress, it also presents complex challenges that require deep ethical and philosophical reflection. How we address these challenges will determine not only the future of technology but also the future of humanity itself.

AI is not just a technical issue—it is a human issue. Recognizing this will allow us to build a future where artificial and human intelligence coexist and collaborate, creating a world that is fairer, more prosperous, and more inclusive.

Shaping Europe's Digital Future

Regulation (EU) 2024/1689 of the European Parliament and the Council Dated June 13, 2024

Establishing harmonized rules on artificial intelligence and amending regulations (EC) No. 300/2008, (EU) No. 167/2013, (EU) No. 168/2013, (EU) 2018/858, (EU) 2018/1139, and (EU) 2019/2144, as well as directives 2014/90/EU, (EU) 2016/797, and (EU) 2020/1828.

(Artificial Intelligence Regulation)

A new intelligence.

Deep mind

Appendix

Glossary of Key Terms

Algorithm
A set of instructions or rules that a computer follows to perform a task or solve a problem. Algorithms are the foundation of all artificial intelli gence applications. (See QR code on page 19)

Machine Learning
A subset of AI that relies on algorithms that learn from data and improve their performance over time without being explicitly programmed for each situation.

Supervised Learning
A type of machine learning in which the model is trained on a dataset of inputs associated with correct outputs, allowing it to learn how to predict the correct result for new data.

Unsupervised Learning
A machine learning method in which the model identifies patterns or structures within data without being given predefined outputs or labels.

Deep Learning
A branch of machine learning that uses deep neural networks—models with many layers of artificial neurons—to analyze and interpret large amounts of complex data.

Neural Network
A mathematical model inspired by the functioning of the human brain, composed of artificial neurons (processing units), used to recognize patterns and solve complex problems.

General Artificial Intelligence (AGI)
A hypothetical type of artificial intelligence capable of understanding, learning, and applying knowledge across a wide range of tasks, similar to human intelligence.

Superintelligence
An advanced form of AI that far exceeds human intelligence in all fields, including creativity and decision-making.

Generative Adversarial Networks (GANs)
A type of machine learning model consisting of two competing neural networks: one generates data (such as images), while the other attempts to distinguish generated data from real data, improving both in the process.

Algorithmic Bias
Bias embedded in algorithms that can arise from imbalanced training data or errors in system design, leading to unfair decisions or outcomes.

Natural Language Processing (NLP)
A field of AI focused on the interaction between computers and human language, enabling machines to understand, interpret, and generate natural language.

Regression
A supervised learning method used to predict continuous values (e.g., estimating the price of a house based on various factors).

Clustering
An unsupervised learning method that automatically groups similar data without prior knowledge of data categories.

Big Data
Large and complex datasets that require advanced processing methods for analysis. AI is often used to extract valuable insights from big data.

Reinforcement Learning
A machine learning method in which an agent learns to take actions in an environment to maximize a reward, using a trial-and-error approach.

List of Recommended Resources

Online Courses
Coursera – "Machine Learning" by Andrew Ng
An introductory course on machine learning, covering fundamental concepts and including hands-on exercises.

edX – "Artificial Intelligence" by MIT
An advanced AI course covering a wide range of topics, from knowledge representation to robotics.

Udemy – "Python for Data Science and Machine Learning Bootcamp"
A practical course on Python and machine learning, ideal for beginners in AI.

Fast.ai – "Practical Deep Learning for Coders"
A free, hands-on course designed to teach how to build deep learning models.

Recommended Books: these books cover technical, philosophical, and ethical aspects of AI, offering a comprehensive perspective on the subject.

Artificial Intelligence: A Guide for Thinking Humans
Melanie Mitchell
Melanie Mitchell – Professor at the Santa Fe Institute
An accessible and critical introduction to artificial intelligence, exploring both its potential and current limitations. Mitchell explains key AI concepts, including machine learning, neural networks, and deep learning, with a focus on what "intelligence" truly means.

Human Compatible:
Artificial Intelligence and the Problem of Control – Stuart Russell
Stuart Russell – Professor at the University of California, Berkeley
Russell discusses the issue of AI safety and argues that artificial intelligence must be designed to be aligned with human objectives. The book analyzes the implications of advanced AI and how to ensure it remains under human control.

The Master Algorithm: How the Quest for the Ultimate Learning Machine Will Remake Our World" – Pedro Domingos
Pedro Domingos – Professor at the University of Washington

A book that explores the concept of a universal algorithm, capable of learning anything from any kind of data. Domingos guides readers through the major schools of machine learning thought and their impact on the future of science and society.

Deep Learning
Ian Goodfellow, Yoshua Bengio, Aaron Courville
Former researcher at Google Brain
Yoshua Bengio – Professor at the University of Montréal
Aaron Courville – Professor at the University of Montréal
A technical textbook that covers the fundamentals of deep learning, from neural networks to generative models. It is considered a must-read for students and researchers in the field of artificial intelligence.

The Alignment Problem:
Machine Learning and Human Values" – Brian Christian
Brian Christian – Research affiliate at the University of California, Berkeley
An in-depth analysis of the AI alignment problem, exploring the ethical and technical challenges of designing artificial intelligence systems that understand and respect human intentions.

Superintelligence
Paths, Dangers, Strategies
Nick Bostrom
Un'esplorazione filosofica dei rischi e delle opportunità dell'intelligenza artificiale avanzata.
Platforms and Tools
Google Colab
A free cloud-based development environment for running Python scripts, ideal for working on machine learning and deep learning projects.

Kaggle
A platform for machine learning competitions, offering free datasets and community-shared notebooks.

TensorFlow
An open-source deep learning framework used to build and train neural networks.

PyTorch
A deep learning framework known for its flexibility and ease of use, particularly popular in academic research.

American online communities dedicated to artificial intelligence:

Association for the Advancement of Artificial Intelligence (AAAI)
AAAI is a leading scientific society dedicated to advancing the under-standing of the mechanisms behind intelligent thought and behavior and their implementation in machines. It organizes conferences, symposia, and publishes the AI Magazine to promote research and education in AI. (aaai.org)

AI LA Community
Based in Los Angeles, AI LA is a community that supports research, development, ethical application, and public education on artificial intel-ligence and emerging technologies. It organizes events, educational programs, and reading groups to promote responsible understanding of AI. (joinai.la)

Partnership on AI
This organization brings together leading companies, organizations, and individuals interested in artificial intelligence to establish common ground and promote responsible practices in the AI ecosystem. It serves as a unifying force for the good of AI. (partnershiponai.org)

Community of Practice: Artificial Intelligence
Managed by the U.S. General Services Administration, this community serves as a network for government employees involved in or interested in artificial intelligence. It offers events, working groups, and training sessions to accelerate responsible AI adoption in government. (coe.gsa.-gov)

OpenAI
OpenAI is a research organization focused on developing and promoting friendly artificial intelligence for the benefit of humanity. It provides a platform for researchers and developers to collaborate and share AI advancements. (openai.com)

These communities provide valuable resources for anyone interested in artificial intelligence, from academic research to practical applications and ethical considerations.

Final Thoughts

As I believe has become quite clear, I am truly enthusiastic about various aspects of technology—even those that seem uncertain or potentially dangerous.

However, I always feel a subtle discomfort knowing that every move I make online is constantly, albeit intelligently, tracked to offer me a product or service that initially boasts the magic word "free", only to later, almost magically, become paid.

For example, when I see "music recommended for you", I can't help but feel that my curiosity is being confined to my habits, depriving me of the small yet wonderful surprise of stumbling upon something entirely different, something far beyond my usual tastes—perhaps expanding my knowledge in unexpected ways.

But what if I don't want recommendations tailored to my habits?

What if I want to randomly come across a Gregorian chant or a Hungarian Csárdás by Béla Bartók?

Could it be that, due to our online choices, we are shaping a flat normality, a neat, clean, and reassuringly straight line?

It would be ideal to have a little "button in the top right corner" allowing us to adjust our level of freedom from AI recommendations:

> *Level 5 → Maximum recommendations*
> *Level 1 → Minimal recommendations, meaning more freedom*

While we wait for this magical button, we can—and indeed, we must—inform ourselves, explore, and experiment, to break free from the flat line of our habitual profile.

The only true wisdom is knowing that you know nothing.

Socrate

www.ingramcontent.com/pod-product-compliance
Lightning Source LLC
LaVergne TN
LVHW052307060326
832902LV00021B/3740